INTRODUCTION TO PURSUING A CAREER IN COMMERCE

Choosing a career in commerce opens a world of opportunities in various sectors such as finance, accounting, business management, and economics. Commerce is the backbone of any economy, involving the study of trade, business activities, financial systems, and economic policies. It equips students with the knowledge and skills to navigate the complexities of the business world and contribute to economic growth and development.

A career in commerce offers a blend of theoretical knowledge and practical skills that are essential in today's dynamic business environment. It prepares individuals to tackle real-world challenges and excel in various professional roles. With continuous learning and professional development, a commerce graduate can achieve significant success and contribute to the growth and stability of the economy.

Why Choose Commerce?

1. **Diverse Career Opportunities**: A degree in commerce offers a wide range of career paths in various industries including banking, finance, insurance, accounting, and consulting. The skills acquired can be applied in both the public and private sectors.

2. **Strong Foundation**: Commerce education provides a strong foundation in core subjects such as accounting, finance, economics, and business law. This knowledge is essential for understanding the functioning of businesses and economies.

3. **Professional Growth**: With a commerce background, you can pursue professional certifications like CA, CS, CMA, CFA, and ACCA, which are highly valued in the job market and can lead to lucrative and prestigious careers.

4. **Global Opportunities**: Commerce graduates are in demand globally. The skills and knowledge acquired are transferable across countries, allowing for international career opportunities.

5. **Entrepreneurial Skills**: A commerce education fosters entrepreneurial thinking and skills. It prepares you to start and manage your own business successfully by understanding market dynamics, financial management, and strategic planning.

KEY AREAS OF STUDY

1. **Accounting**: Understanding financial statements, auditing, and financial reporting.
2. **Finance**: Knowledge of financial markets, investment strategies, and risk management.
3. **Economics**: Studying microeconomics and macroeconomics to understand market behavior and economic policies.
4. **Business Management**: Learning management principles, organizational behavior, and strategic management.
5. **Marketing**: Understanding consumer behavior, market research, and advertising strategies.

INTRODUCTION TO COURSES ALONGSIDE OR AFTER BCOM

In today's competitive and dynamic job market, a Bachelor of Commerce (BCom) degree serves as a strong foundation for a myriad of career opportunities. However, to stand out and excel in specialized fields, many students opt to pursue additional courses alongside or after completing their BCom. These courses can enhance their expertise, open new career pathways, and provide a significant edge in their professional journey.

In this book, we will explore in detail the various courses that can be pursued along with or after a BCom degree. Whether you are looking to deepen your knowledge in a specific area of commerce, expand your skills in business management, or explore new fields like data analytics and digital marketing, we will cover a wide range of options tailored to meet diverse career aspirations.

From professional certifications like Chartered Accountancy (CA) and Chartered Financial Analyst (CFA) to postgraduate degrees such as Master of Commerce (MCom) and Master of Business Administration (MBA), we will delve into the specifics of each course, including the curriculum, career prospects, and the advantages they offer. Additionally, we will look at short-term diploma and certificate programs that provide focused training in areas like taxation, banking, and financial planning.

In this book, we will explore in detail the various courses that can be pursued along with or after a BCom degree. Whether you are looking to deepen your knowledge in a specific area of commerce, expand your skills in business management, or explore new fields like data analytics and digital marketing, we will cover a wide range of options tailored to meet diverse career aspirations.

The following are the courses that can be undertaken by commerce graduates or students:

- **Professional Certifications:**
    1. **Chartered Accountancy (CA):** One of the most prestigious and challenging courses, focusing on auditing, taxation, and accounting.
    2. **Company Secretary (CS):** Specializes in corporate law, governance, and secretarial practices.
    3. **Cost and Management Accountancy (CMA):** Focuses on cost management, financial planning, and business strategy.
    4. **Certified Public Accountant (CPA):** Globally recognized certification in

accounting and finance.
5. **Certified Management Accountant (CMA - US):** Focuses on financial management and strategic planning.
6. **Association of Chartered Certified Accountants (ACCA):** Global qualification covering financial management, taxation, and auditing.
7. **Chartered Financial Analyst (CFA):** Focuses on investment management, financial analysis, and portfolio management.

- **Postgraduate Courses:**
1. **Master of Commerce (MCom):** Advanced studies in commerce, focusing on various aspects of business and finance.
2. **Master of Business Administration (MBA):** Specializations available in finance, marketing, human resources, operations, and more.
3. **Master of Financial Management (MFM):** Focuses on advanced financial management concepts and practices.
4. **Master of Economics:** Advanced study in economic theory, econometrics, and applied economics.
5. **Master of Management Studies (MMS):** Similar to an MBA, focusing on managerial and business skills.

- **Diploma and Certificate Courses**
1. **Diploma in Banking and Finance:** Specialized knowledge in banking operations, financial services, and regulations.
2. **Certificate in Investment Banking:** Focuses on investment banking, mergers and acquisitions, and financial analysis.
3. **Diploma in Taxation:** In-depth knowledge of tax laws and practices.
4. **Certificate in Financial Planning (CFP):** Focuses on financial planning, investment management, and retirement planning.

- **Information Technology and Data Analytics**
1. **Certified Information Systems Auditor (CISA):** Certification in auditing, control, and security of information systems.
2. **Certified Information Security Manager (CISM):** Focuses on information security management.
3. **Data Analytics and Business Intelligence Courses:** Specialized courses in data analysis, machine learning, and business intelligence tools.

We will see them course by course, providing detailed explanations of each, highlighting their key components, learning outcomes, and the career pathways they open up. By understanding these educational pathways, you will be better equipped to make informed decisions about your career development and maximize the potential of your BCom degree. Join us as we navigate through the myriad of courses that can complement your commerce education and propel you toward a successful and fulfilling career.

PROFESSIONAL CERTIFICATIONS

First, we will look into professional certifications, which are designed to provide specialized knowledge and skills that are highly valued in the job market. These certifications can significantly enhance your career prospects by demonstrating your expertise and commitment to continuous learning. Here are some of the most sought-after professional certifications for commerce graduates:

CHARTERED ACCOUNTANCY (CA):

Overview: Chartered Accountancy is one of the most prestigious and challenging certifications in the field of accounting and finance. It covers various aspects of auditing, taxation, and financial reporting.

Eligibility Criteria:
1. **Foundation Course:** After completing Class 12th or its equivalent from a recognized board, you can register for the CA Foundation course.
2. **Direct Entry Route:** If you are a graduate or postgraduate in commerce with a minimum of 55% marks or other graduates or postgraduates with a minimum of 60% marks, you can directly enter the Intermediate course without appearing for the Foundation course.
3. **ICAI Intermediate Examination (Existing Scheme):** Commerce graduates/postgraduates with a minimum of 55% marks or other graduates/postgraduates with a minimum of 60% marks can register directly for the Intermediate course without appearing for the Foundation course.

Intermediate Course Structure:
1. **Articleship:** After clearing either or both groups of the Intermediate examination, you need to register for a three-year articleship under a practicing chartered accountant.
2. **Integrated Course on Information Technology and Soft Skills (ICITSS):** Before appearing in the CA Final examination, you need to complete the ICITSS course comprising Information Technology (IT) and Orientation Program.
3. **Final Course:** After passing both groups of the Intermediate examination and completing the articleship, you can register for the CA Final course.

CA Final Examination:
- After completing the Final course, you can appear for the CA Final examination.

Membership:
- Upon passing the CA Final examination and completing the required practical training, you can become a member of ICAI and use the designation of a Chartered Accountant.

Job Opportunities:

Chartered Accountants (CAs) have a wide range of job opportunities across various industries and sectors. Here are some common job roles for CAs:

1. **Audit Manager**: Responsible for planning and overseeing audits, ensuring compliance with regulations, and providing recommendations for improvement.
2. **Tax Manager**: Manages tax planning and compliance for individuals and businesses, ensuring compliance with tax laws and regulations.
3. **Financial Controller**: Manages the financial operations of an organization, including financial reporting, budgeting, and internal controls.
4. **Chief Financial Officer (CFO)**: Responsible for overseeing the financial operations of a company, including financial planning, reporting, and risk management.
5. **Management Accountant**: Provides financial analysis and support to management for decision-making purposes.
6. **Financial Analyst**: Analyzes financial data and trends to provide insights and recommendations to stakeholders.
7. **Forensic Accountant**: Investigates financial fraud and misconduct, providing litigation support and expert testimony.
8. **Consultant**: Provides financial and strategic advice to clients on a range of issues, such as mergers and acquisitions, restructuring, and financial planning.
9. **Internal Auditor**: Evaluates and improves the effectiveness of internal controls, risk management processes, and governance frameworks within an organization.
10. **Academician**: Teaches accounting and finance courses and conducts research in accounting and related fields.

CHARTERED FINANCIAL ANALYST (CFA):

Overview: The CFA designation is highly respected in the investment management and financial analysis sectors. It focuses on investment analysis, portfolio management, and ethical standards. It is offered by the CFA Institute and is highly respected in the industry. Here's a guide to joining the CFA program and its eligibility requirements:

Eligibility Criteria:
1. **Education**: You must have a bachelor's degree or equivalent education (or be in the final year of your bachelor's degree program) or have four years of qualified, professional work experience or a combination of work and college experience that totals at least four years.
2. **Work Experience:** You must have a minimum of four years of professional work experience in investment decision-making.
3. **Membership:** You must become a member of the CFA Institute and agree to adhere to the CFA Institute Code of Ethics and Standards of Professional Conduct.

Registration Process:
1. **Create an Account:** Visit the CFA Institute website (www.cfainstitute.org) and create an account.
2. **Determine Eligibility:** Check if you meet the eligibility criteria for the CFA program.
3. **Register for the Exam:** Register for the CFA exam by selecting a test center and paying the exam fees.
4. **Prepare for the Exam**: Study for the exam using the CFA Institute's recommended study materials or other preparatory resources.
5. **Take the Exam:** Sit for the CFA exam at the designated test center.
6. **Pass the Exam**: Pass all three levels of the CFA exam to earn the CFA charter.

CFA Program Structure:
1. **Level I:** Focuses on tools and concepts related to investment valuation and portfolio management. It consists of multiple-choice questions.
2. **Level II**: Focuses on the application of valuation concepts in a real-world setting.

It consists of item set questions.
3. **Level III:** Focuses on synthesizing all the concepts and analytical methods in a variety of applications for effective portfolio management and wealth planning. It consists of essay questions and item set questions.
4. **Work Experience:** After passing all three levels of the exam, you must complete four years of qualified, professional work experience before receiving the CFA charter.

Job opportunities:

Chartered Financial Analysts (CFAs) have a wide range of job opportunities in the finance and investment industry. Here are some common job roles for CFAs:

1. **Portfolio Manager:** Manages investment portfolios for individuals or institutions, making investment decisions to achieve financial goals.
2. **Research Analyst:** Conducts financial research and analysis to provide investment recommendations and insights.
3. **Risk Manager:** Identifies and manages financial risks within an organization, such as market risk, credit risk, and operational risk.
4. **Investment Banker:** Provides financial advisory services for mergers and acquisitions, capital raising, and other financial transactions.
5. **Financial Advisor:** Provides investment advice and financial planning services to clients, helping them achieve their financial goals.
6. **Asset Manager:** Manages assets, such as stocks, bonds, and real estate, on behalf of clients or institutions.
7. **Hedge Fund Manager:** Manages a hedge fund, making investment decisions to generate returns for investors.
8. **Private Equity Analyst:** Analyzes investment opportunities in private companies and manages investments in private equity funds.
9. **Corporate Finance Analyst:** Provides financial analysis and support for corporate finance activities, such as financial planning, budgeting, and capital budgeting.
10. **Financial Consultant:** Provides financial advice and consulting services to clients on a range of financial matters.

COMPANY SECRETARY (CS):

Overview: The Company Secretary certification specializes in corporate governance, company law, and secretarial practices. It is essential for ensuring legal compliance and effective administration in corporate entities. Becoming a Company Secretary (CS) is a prestigious and rewarding career path in the field of corporate governance and compliance. The Institute of Company Secretaries of India (ICSI) regulates and conducts the CS course. Here's a guide to joining the CS course and its eligibility requirements:

Eligibility Criteria:
1. **Foundation Course**: After completing Class 12th or its equivalent from a recognized board, you can register for the CS Foundation course.
2. **Executive Programme (Direct Entry)**: If you are a graduate or postgraduate in commerce with a minimum of 50% marks, or have a degree in any other discipline with a minimum of 55% marks, you can directly enter the Executive Programme without appearing for the Foundation course.
3. **Professional Programme (After Executive Programme)**: After clearing the Executive Programme, you can register for the Professional Programme.

Executive Programme Structure:
1. **Registration:** Register for the Executive Programme after completing the Foundation course or meeting the direct entry eligibility criteria.
2. **Modules:** The Executive Programme consists of two modules, each covering various subjects related to corporate law, management, taxation, and accounting.
3. **Examinations:** After completing the study material for each module, you can appear for the respective module exams conducted by ICSI.

Professional Programme:
1. **Registration:** Register for the Professional Programme after clearing both modules of the Executive Programme.
2. **Modules:** The Professional Programme consists of three modules, covering advanced topics in corporate law, governance, secretarial practice, and management.
3. **Examinations:** After completing the study material for each module, you can appear for the respective module exams conducted by ICSI.

Practical Training:

1. **Training Requirement:** After clearing the Executive Programme, you need to undergo 15 months of practical training in a company or under a practicing Company Secretary.
2. **Professional Development Programme (PDP):** After completing the Professional Programme, you need to undergo a 15-day Professional Development Programme conducted by ICSI.

Job opportunities:

Company Secretaries (CS) play a crucial role in ensuring that companies comply with statutory and regulatory requirements. Here are some common job opportunities for Company Secretaries:

1. **Company Secretary**: The primary role of a Company Secretary is to ensure that the company complies with legal and regulatory requirements. They also advise the board of directors on corporate governance matters.
2. **Corporate Governance Manager**: Responsible for overseeing the company's corporate governance policies and practices, ensuring compliance with regulations and best practices.
3. **Legal Advisor**: Provides legal advice and support to the company on a range of legal issues, including corporate law, contract law, and regulatory compliance.
4. **Compliance Officer**: Ensures that the company complies with relevant laws, regulations, and internal policies, and monitors compliance-related risks.
5. **Board Support**: Provides support to the board of directors, including organizing board meetings, preparing agendas and minutes, and ensuring compliance with corporate governance requirements.
6. **Risk Manager**: Identifies and manages risks within the company, including legal and regulatory risks, and develops strategies to mitigate these risks.
7. **Company Administrator**: Manages administrative tasks related to the company, such as maintaining corporate records, filing statutory returns, and liaising with regulatory authorities.
8. **Corporate Secretary**: Provides secretarial support to the company, including managing correspondence, maintaining records, and organizing meetings.
9. **Legal Compliance Officer**: Ensures that the company complies with all applicable laws and regulations, including those related to corporate governance, ethics, and disclosure.
10. **Corporate Counsel**: Provides legal advice and representation to the company on legal matters, including litigation, contracts, and regulatory compliance.

COST AND MANAGEMENT ACCOUNTANCY (CMA):

Overview: The CMA certification focuses on cost management, financial planning, and business strategy. It equips professionals with skills to enhance business efficiency and financial performance. The Cost and Management Accountancy (CMA) course is ideal for those interested in cost management, financial planning, and business strategy. It is offered by the Institute of Cost Accountants of India (ICMAI). Here's a guide to joining the CMA course and its eligibility requirements:

Eligibility Criteria:
1. **Foundation Course**: After completing Class 12th or its equivalent from a recognized board, you can register for the CMA Foundation course.
2. **Direct Entry Route**: If you are a graduate or postgraduate in commerce with a minimum of 50% marks, or have a degree in any other discipline with a minimum of 60% marks, you can directly enter the Intermediate course without appearing for the Foundation course.
3. **ICAI Intermediate Examination (Existing Scheme)**: Commerce graduates/ postgraduates with a minimum of 55% marks or other graduates/ postgraduates with a minimum of 60% marks can register directly for the Intermediate course without appearing for the Foundation course.

Registration Process:
1. **Visit the ICMAI Website**: Go to the official website of the Institute of Cost Accountants of India (ICMAI) at www.icmai.in.
2. **Create a Student Account**: Register yourself as a student by creating an account on the ICMAI portal.
3. **Submit Required Documents**: Upload scanned copies of your photograph, signature, and educational documents as per the eligibility criteria.
4. **Pay the Registration Fee**: Pay the prescribed registration fee online through the ICMAI portal.
5. **Receive Study Material**: Once your registration is confirmed, you will receive the study material for the course.

Intermediate Course Structure:
1. **Articleship**: After clearing either or both groups of the Intermediate

examination, you need to register for a three-year articleship under a practicing cost accountant.
2. **Integrated Course on Information Technology and Soft Skills (ICITSS)**: Before appearing in the CMA Final examination, you need to complete the ICITSS course comprising Information Technology (IT) and Orientation Program.
3. **Final Course**: After passing both groups of the Intermediate examination and completing the articleship, you can register for the CMA Final course.

CMA Final Examination:
- After completing the Final course, you can appear for the CMA Final examination.

Membership:
- Upon passing the CMA Final examination and completing the required practical training, you can become a member of ICMAI and use the designation of a Cost and Management Accountant.

Job opportunities:
Cost and Management Accountants (CMAs) play a critical role in helping organizations make informed business decisions by providing financial expertise and analysis. Here are some common job opportunities for CMAs:
1. **Cost Accountant**: Responsible for analyzing costs, preparing cost reports, and advising management on cost-efficient practices.
2. **Management Accountant**: Provides financial analysis and support to management for decision-making purposes, including budgeting, forecasting, and performance analysis.
3. **Financial Analyst**: Analyzes financial data and trends to provide insights and recommendations to stakeholders, including management and investors.
4. **Budget Analyst**: Prepares and analyzes budgets, monitors spending, and provides recommendations to ensure that budgets are adhered to.
5. **Financial Manager**: Oversees the financial operations of an organization, including financial reporting, budgeting, and forecasting.
6. **Controller**: Manages the accounting operations of an organization, including the production of financial reports, maintenance of accounting records, and ensuring compliance with regulations.
7. **Internal Auditor**: Evaluates and improves the effectiveness of internal controls, risk management processes, and governance frameworks within an organization.
8. **Cost Estimator**: Calculates the costs of goods or services based on analysis of data, market trends, and other factors.
9. **Financial Consultant**: Provides financial advice and consulting services to clients on a range of issues, such as cost management, financial planning, and

performance improvement.
10. **Project Accountant**: Manages the financial aspects of projects, including budgeting, cost tracking, and financial reporting.

CERTIFIED PUBLIC ACCOUNTANT (CPA):

Overview: The Certified Public Accountant (CPA) designation is highly respected in the field of accounting and finance. It is offered by the American Institute of Certified Public Accountants (AICPA) and administered by the National Association of State Boards of Accountancy (NASBA). Here's a guide to joining the CPA program and its eligibility requirements:

Eligibility Criteria:
1. **Education:** You must have a bachelor's degree or equivalent education from a regionally accredited institution.
2. **Accounting Courses:** You must have completed a minimum number of accounting courses, which may vary by state. Typically, these include courses in financial accounting, auditing, taxation, and management accounting.
3. **Business Courses:** Some states require you to have completed a certain number of business courses, such as economics, finance, and business law.
4. **Work Experience:** Most states require you to have a certain amount of professional accounting experience, usually around 1-2 years, supervised by a licensed CPA.

CPA Exam:
- You must pass the Uniform CPA Examination, which is a four-part exam covering auditing and attestation, business environment and concepts, financial accounting and reporting, and regulation.

Ethics Exam:
- Some states require you to pass an ethics exam, such as the AICPA Professional Ethics Exam, to become licensed as a CPA.

Registration Process:
1. **Check State Requirements:** Determine the specific requirements for CPA licensure in the state where you plan to practice, as they can vary.
2. **Apply for CPA Exam:** Submit an application to take the CPA Exam through the NASBA or your state board of accountancy.
3. **Schedule Exam:** Once your application is approved, schedule your exam with a

Prometric testing center.
4. **Study for Exam:** Prepare for the exam using review courses and study materials recommended by the AICPA and NASBA.
5. **Take Exam:** Sit for the CPA Exam at the scheduled date and time.
6. **Pass Exam:** Pass all four parts of the CPA Exam within a certain period (usually 18 months to 3 years, depending on the state).
7. **Apply for License:** After passing the CPA Exam and meeting the work experience requirements, apply for your CPA license through your state board of accountancy.

Job opportunities:

Certified Public Accountants (CPAs) have a wide range of job opportunities in accounting, finance, and business. Here are some common job roles for CPAs:

1. **Public Accountant**: Provides accounting, tax, auditing, and consulting services to individuals, businesses, and government agencies.
2. **Auditor**: Examines financial statements and accounting records to ensure accuracy and compliance with laws and regulations.
3. **Tax Advisor/Consultant**: Provides tax planning and compliance services to individuals and businesses, helping them minimize their tax liabilities and comply with tax laws.
4. **Financial Analyst**: Analyzes financial data and trends to provide insights and recommendations to stakeholders.
5. **Financial Manager**: Oversees the financial operations of an organization, including financial reporting, budgeting, and forecasting.
6. **Controller**: Manages the accounting operations of an organization, including the production of financial reports, maintenance of accounting records, and ensuring compliance with regulations.
7. **Forensic Accountant**: Investigates financial fraud and misconduct, providing litigation support and expert testimony.
8. **Internal Auditor**: Evaluates and improves the effectiveness of internal controls, risk management processes, and governance frameworks within an organization.
9. **Chief Financial Officer (CFO)**: Responsible for overseeing the financial operations of a company, including financial planning, reporting, and risk management.
10. **Academician**: Teaches accounting and finance courses and conducts research in accounting and related fields.

CERTIFIED MANAGEMENT ACCOUNTANT (CMA - US):

Overview: The Certified Management Accountant (CMA) certification is offered by the Institute of Management Accountants (IMA) and is a globally recognized credential for management accountants. Here's a guide to joining the CMA program and its eligibility requirements:

Eligibility Criteria:
1. **Education:** You must have a bachelor's degree from an accredited college or university or a related professional certification. A degree in accounting, finance, or business is preferred but not required.
2. **Membership:** You must become a member of the Institute of Management Accountants (IMA) to access the CMA program and its benefits.
3. **Work Experience:** You must have two continuous years of professional experience in management accounting or financial management. This requirement can be completed before or within seven years of passing the CMA exam.

Registration Process:
1. **Visit the IMA Website:** Go to the official website of the Institute of Management Accountants (IMA) at www.imanet.org.
2. **Create an Account:** Register yourself as a member of IMA and create an account on the IMA portal.
3. **Submit Required Documents:** Upload scanned copies of your educational transcripts and other supporting documents as per the eligibility criteria.
4. **Pay the Registration Fee:** Pay the prescribed registration fee for the CMA program online through the IMA portal.
5. **Receive Study Material:** Once your registration is confirmed, you will receive the study material for the CMA exam.

CMA Program Structure:
1. **CMA Exam:** The CMA exam consists of two parts – Part 1: Financial Reporting, Planning, Performance, and Control, and Part 2: Financial Decision Making. Each part has a duration of four hours.

2. **Exam Preparation:** Study for the exam using the IMA's recommended study materials, review courses, and practice exams.
3. **Exam Registration:** Register for each part of the CMA exam separately through the IMA portal and schedule your exam at a Prometric testing center.
4. **Passing the Exam:** Pass both parts of the CMA exam within three years of entering the program to earn the CMA certification.
5. **Continuing Education:** Maintain your CMA certification by completing 30 hours of continuing education each year, including two hours of ethics education.

Job Opportunities:

Certified Management Accountants (CMAs) in the United States have a variety of job opportunities in accounting, finance, and business. Here are some common job roles for CMAs:

1. **Financial Analyst**: Analyzes financial data and trends to provide insights and recommendations to stakeholders.
2. **Cost Accountant**: Analyzes costs, prepares cost reports, and advises management on cost-efficient practices.
3. **Budget Analyst**: Prepares and analyzes budgets, monitors spending, and provides recommendations to ensure budgets are adhered to.
4. **Internal Auditor**: Evaluates and improves the effectiveness of internal controls, risk management processes, and governance frameworks within an organization.
5. **Management Accountant**: Provides financial analysis and support to management for decision-making purposes.
6. **Financial Manager**: Oversees the financial operations of an organization, including financial reporting, budgeting, and forecasting.
7. **Controller**: Manages the accounting operations of an organization, including the production of financial reports, maintenance of accounting records, and ensuring compliance with regulations.
8. **Financial Consultant**: Provides financial advice and consulting services to clients on a range of issues, such as cost management, financial planning, and performance improvement.
9. **Chief Financial Officer (CFO)**: Responsible for overseeing the financial operations of a company, including financial planning, reporting, and risk management.
10. **Project Accountant**: Manages the financial aspects of projects, including budgeting, cost tracking, and financial reporting.

ASSOCIATION OF CHARTERED CERTIFIED ACCOUNTANTS (ACCA):

Overview: The Association of Chartered Certified Accountants (ACCA) is a globally recognized professional accounting body offering the Chartered Certified Accountant qualification. Here's a guide to joining the ACCA and its eligibility requirements:

Eligibility Criteria:
1. **Education:** You must have a minimum of three GCSEs and two A levels in five separate subjects, including math and English, or equivalent qualifications.
2. **Exemptions:** If you have a relevant degree or professional qualification, you may be eligible for exemptions from some ACCA exams.
3. **English Language Proficiency:** If English is not your first language, you must demonstrate proficiency through tests like IELTS or TOEFL.

Registration Process:
1. **Visit the ACCA Website:** Go to the official website of the Association of Chartered Certified Accountants (ACCA) at www.accaglobal.com.
2. **Create an Account:** Register yourself as a student by creating an account on the ACCA portal.
3. **Submit Required Documents:** Upload scanned copies of your educational transcripts, proof of identity, and other supporting documents as per the eligibility criteria.
4. **Pay the Registration Fee:** Pay the prescribed registration fee for the ACCA qualification online through the ACCA portal.
5. **Receive Study Material:** Once your registration is confirmed, you will receive the study material for the ACCA exams.

ACCA Qualification Structure:
1. **Knowledge Level:** The first level of the ACCA qualification consists of three papers: Accountant in Business (AB), Management Accounting (MA), and Financial Accounting (FA).
2. **Skills Level:** The second level consists of six papers, divided into two modules:

Essentials and Options. The Essentials module includes papers on Corporate and Business Law (LW), Performance Management (PM), Taxation (TX), and Financial Reporting (FR). The Options module allows you to choose two papers from a list of four.
3. **Professional Level:** The final level consists of three papers: Strategic Business Leader (SBL), Strategic Business Reporting (SBR), and an Options paper. You also need to complete an Ethics and Professional Skills module.
4. **Practical Experience:** In addition to passing the exams, you must complete a minimum of three years of relevant practical experience to become an ACCA member.

Job opportunities:
The Association of Chartered Certified Accountants (ACCA) qualification opens up a wide range of job opportunities in accounting, finance, and business. Here are some common job roles for ACCA professionals:

1. **Financial Accountant:** Responsible for preparing financial statements, ensuring compliance with accounting standards, and providing financial analysis and insights.
2. **Management Accountant:** Provides financial analysis and support to management for decision-making purposes, including budgeting, forecasting, and performance analysis.
3. **Auditor:** Examines financial statements and accounting records to ensure accuracy and compliance with laws and regulations.
4. **Tax Advisor/Consultant:** Provides tax planning and compliance services to individuals and businesses, helping them minimize their tax liabilities and comply with tax laws.
5. **Financial Analyst:** Analyzes financial data and trends to provide insights and recommendations to stakeholders.
6. **Internal Auditor:** Evaluates and improves the effectiveness of internal controls, risk management processes, and governance frameworks within an organization.
7. **Risk Manager:** Identifies and manages financial risks within an organization, such as market risk, credit risk, and operational risk.
8. **Financial Manager:** Oversees the financial operations of an organization, including financial reporting, budgeting, and forecasting.
9. **Chief Financial Officer (CFO):** Responsible for overseeing the financial operations of a company, including financial planning, reporting, and risk management.
10. **Consultant:** Provides financial and strategic advice to clients on a range of issues, such as mergers and acquisitions, restructuring, and financial planning.

POSTGRADUATE COURSES FOR COMMERCE GRADUATES

After completing a Bachelor of Commerce (BCom) degree, many students choose to pursue postgraduate courses to further specialize in a specific area of commerce or to broaden their skills and knowledge base. Here are some of the common postgraduate courses that commerce graduates can consider:

MASTER OF COMMERCE (MCOM)

Overview: The MCom degree is a postgraduate program that focuses on various aspects of commerce such as accounting, economics, finance, and management.

Curriculum: The curriculum typically includes advanced topics in accounting, finance, economics, taxation, business management, and organizational behavior.

Eligibility Criteria:
1. **Education:** You must have a bachelor's degree in commerce (BCom) or a related field from a recognized university. Some universities may require a minimum percentage of marks in the qualifying examination (typically around 50% or higher).
2. **Entrance Exams:** Some universities or colleges may require you to pass an entrance exam, such as the Common Admission Test (CAT), Management Aptitude Test (MAT), or the university's own entrance exam.
3. **Work Experience:** While work experience is not typically required for admission to the MCom program, some universities may give preference to candidates with relevant work experience.

Career Pathways: Graduates with an MCom degree can pursue careers in accounting, finance, banking, consultancy, and academia. They can also opt for roles in corporate finance, investment banking, financial analysis, and management consulting.

MASTER OF BUSINESS ADMINISTRATION (MBA)

Overview: The MBA is a postgraduate degree that provides a comprehensive understanding of business management principles and practices.

Curriculum: The curriculum covers various aspects of business management, including marketing, finance, operations, human resources, and strategy.

Eligibility Criteria:

1. **Education:** You must have a bachelor's degree in any discipline from a recognized university. Some universities may require a minimum percentage of marks in the qualifying examination (typically around 50% or higher).
2. **Work Experience:** While work experience is not always required, many MBA programs prefer candidates with some professional work experience. The required work experience may vary depending on the program and the university.
3. **Entrance Exams:** Many MBA programs require candidates to take entrance exams such as the Common Admission Test (CAT), Management Aptitude Test (MAT), Graduate Management Admission Test (GMAT), or the university's own entrance exam.

Career Pathways:

- MBA graduates can pursue careers in a wide range of industries and sectors, including finance, consulting, technology, healthcare, and entrepreneurship. They often take up leadership roles such as business development managers, project managers, operations directors, and chief executive officers.

MASTER OF ACCOUNTING (MACC)

Overview: The MAcc degree is designed for students who wish to specialize in accounting and pursue careers as professional accountants or auditors.

Curriculum: The curriculum focuses on advanced topics in accounting, auditing, taxation, and financial reporting. It also prepares students for professional accounting certifications such as CPA, CA, and CMA.

Career Pathways: MAcc graduates can pursue careers as certified public accountants (CPAs), auditors, tax consultants, forensic accountants, and financial analysts. They are in high demand in accounting firms, corporations, government agencies, and non-profit organizations.

MASTER OF FINANCE (MFIN)

Overview: The MFin degree is ideal for students interested in financial management, investment analysis, and financial markets.

Curriculum: The curriculum covers topics such as financial theory, quantitative methods, risk management, corporate finance, and investment analysis.

Eligibility Criteria:
1. **Education**: You must have a bachelor's degree in any discipline from a recognized university. Some universities may require a background in finance, accounting, or business-related fields.
2. **Entrance Exams**: Some universities or institutes may require candidates to take entrance exams such as the Common Admission Test (CAT), Management Aptitude Test (MAT), or the university's own entrance exam.

Career Pathways: MFin graduates can pursue careers in investment banking, asset management, corporate finance, financial planning, and risk management. They often work as financial analysts, portfolio managers, investment bankers, and risk managers.

DIPLOMA AND CERTIFICATE COURSES IN COMMERCE

Diploma and certificate courses in commerce offer specialized training in specific areas of business and finance. These courses are designed to provide practical skills and knowledge that can enhance your career prospects. Here are some common diploma and certificate courses in commerce and their benefits:

DIPLOMA IN BANKING AND FINANCE PROGRAM

The Diploma in Banking and Finance program is designed to provide students with a comprehensive understanding of banking and financial services. Here's a guide to joining the program and its eligibility requirements:

Eligibility Criteria:
1. **Education**: You must have completed high school (10+2) or its equivalent from a recognized board or university.
2. **Minimum Marks**: Some institutes may require a minimum percentage of marks in the qualifying examination (typically around 50% or higher).
3. **Entrance Exams**: Some institutes may conduct entrance exams to assess the candidate's aptitude for the program.

Job Opportunities:
1. **Banking Sector:** You can work in various roles in banks, such as bank teller, customer service representative, loan officer, or branch manager.
2. **Financial Services:** You can work in financial services firms, insurance companies, or investment firms in roles such as financial advisor, investment analyst, or insurance agent.
3. **Government Sector:** You can explore job opportunities in government banks, regulatory bodies, or government financial institutions.
4. **Corporate Sector:** You can work in the finance departments of companies in roles such as financial analyst, finance manager, or treasury manager.

CERTIFICATE IN INVESTMENT BANKING PROGRAM

The Certificate in Investment Banking is a specialized program that provides training in investment banking principles and practices. Here's a guide to joining the program and its eligibility requirements:

Eligibility Criteria:
1. **Education:** You must have completed high school (10+2) or its equivalent from a recognized board or university.
2. **Minimum Marks:** Some institutes may require a minimum percentage of marks in the qualifying examination (typically around 50% or higher).

Job Opportunities:
1. **Investment Banking Firms:** You can work in investment banking firms in roles such as investment banking analyst, associate, or manager.
2. **Financial Institutions:** You can work in financial institutions such as banks, insurance companies, or asset management firms in roles related to investment banking.
3. **Corporate Finance:** You can work in the finance departments of companies in roles such as financial analyst, finance manager, or treasury manager with a focus on investment banking activities.
4. **Consulting Firms:** You can work in consulting firms that provide advisory services to clients in areas such as mergers and acquisitions, corporate finance, and capital raising.

DIPLOMA IN TAXATION PROGRAM

The Diploma in Taxation is a specialized program that provides training in tax laws, regulations, and practices. Here's a guide to joining the program and its eligibility requirements:

Eligibility Criteria:
1. **Education:** You must have completed high school (10+2) or its equivalent from a recognized board or university.
2. **Minimum Marks:** Some institutes may require a minimum percentage of marks in the qualifying examination (typically around 50% or higher).

Job Opportunities:
1. **Tax Consultancy Firms:** You can work in tax consultancy firms in roles such as tax consultant, tax advisor, or tax analyst.
2. **Accounting Firms:** You can work in accounting firms in roles such as tax accountant, tax auditor, or tax manager.
3. **Corporate Tax Departments:** You can work in the tax departments of corporations in roles such as tax analyst, tax specialist, or tax manager.
4. **Government Tax Agencies:** You can work in government tax agencies in roles related to tax administration, tax enforcement, or tax policy analysis.

CERTIFICATE IN FINANCIAL PLANNING (CFP) PROGRAM

The Certificate in Financial Planning (CFP) is a professional certification program that provides training in financial planning principles and practices. Here's a guide to joining the program and its eligibility requirements:

Eligibility Criteria:
1. **Education:** You must have completed high school (10+2) or its equivalent from a recognized board or university.
2. **Minimum Age:** Some institutes may require candidates to be at least 21 years old.

Job Opportunities:
1. **Financial Planning Firms:** You can work in financial planning firms in roles such as financial planner, wealth manager, or investment advisor.
2. **Financial Institutions:** You can work in banks, insurance companies, or asset management firms in roles related to financial planning and advisory.
3. **Independent Practice:** You can start your own financial planning practice and offer services to individual clients or businesses.
4. **Consulting Firms:** You can work in consulting firms that provide financial planning services to clients.

INFORMATION TECHNOLOGY (IT) AND DATA ANALYTICS:

Studying Information Technology and Data Analytics alongside a BCom degree can provide you with a strong foundation in both business and technology, opening up a world of opportunities in today's digital economy. The combination of these skills will equip you to succeed in a variety of roles that require a deep understanding of business operations, technology, and data analysis.

CERTIFIED INFORMATION SYSTEMS AUDITOR (CISA) PROGRAM

The Certified Information Systems Auditor (CISA) certification is a globally recognized certification for information systems audit control, assurance, and security professionals. Here's a guide to joining the program and its eligibility requirements:

Eligibility Criteria:
1. **Experience:** You must have a minimum of five years of professional information systems auditing, control, or security work experience. However, a maximum of three years can be waived based on certain education and experience substitutions.
2. **Education:** A minimum of a bachelor's degree from an accredited university is required. However, a maximum of one year of this requirement can be waived based on certain education and experience substitutions.
3. **Adherence to the Code of Professional Ethics:** You must adhere to the ISACA Code of Professional Ethics.

Registration Process:
1. **Register for the Exam:** Visit the ISACA website and register for the CISA exam. You will need to pay the exam fee at this stage.
2. **Prepare for the Exam:** Study for the exam using official ISACA resources, review courses, and practice exams.
3. **Schedule the Exam:** Once you feel prepared, schedule your exam through the ISACA website or a local testing center.
4. **Take the Exam:** On the day of the exam, arrive at the testing center on time and complete the exam according to the instructions provided.
5. **Receive Your Score:** You will receive your exam score immediately upon completion of the exam.
6. **Apply for Certification:** Once you have passed the exam and met the experience and education requirements, you can apply for certification through the ISACA website.

Job Opportunities:
1. **IT Auditor:** Conduct audits of information systems, practices, and operations to ensure compliance with policies and regulations.
2. **Information Security Manager:** Develop and implement security policies and procedures to protect information assets.
3. **Risk Manager:** Identify and manage risks related to information systems and technology.
4. **IT Consultant:** Provide advice and guidance to organizations on information systems and technology issues.
5. **Compliance Officer:** Ensure that organizations comply with relevant laws, regulations, and standards related to information systems and technology.

CERTIFIED INFORMATION SECURITY MANAGER (CISM) PROGRAM

The Certified Information Security Manager (CISM) certification is a globally recognized certification for information security professionals. Here's a guide to joining the program and its eligibility requirements:

Eligibility Criteria:
1. **Experience:** You must have a minimum of five years of experience in information security management, with a minimum of three years of experience in three or more of the job practice analysis areas.
2. **Adherence to the Code of Professional Ethics:** You must adhere to the ISACA Code of Professional Ethics.

Registration Process:
1. **Register for the Exam:** Visit the ISACA website and register for the CISM exam. You will need to pay the exam fee at this stage.
2. **Prepare for the Exam:** Study for the exam using official ISACA resources, review courses, and practice exams.
3. **Schedule the Exam:** Once you feel prepared, schedule your exam through the ISACA website or a local testing center.
4. **Take the Exam:** On the day of the exam, arrive at the testing center on time and complete the exam according to the instructions provided.
5. **Receive Your Score:** You will receive your exam score immediately upon completion of the exam.
6. **Apply for Certification:** Once you have passed the exam and met the experience requirements, you can apply for certification through the ISACA website.

Job Opportunities:
1. **Information Security Manager**: Manage and oversee an organization's information security program.
2. **Chief Information Security Officer (CISO)**: Lead the organization's information security strategy and implementation.

3. **Security Consultant**: Provide advice and guidance to organizations on information security issues.
4. **Risk Manager**: Identify and manage risks related to information security.
5. **Compliance Officer**: Ensure that organizations comply with relevant laws, regulations, and standards related to information security.

DATA ANALYTICS AND BUSINESS INTELLIGENCE COURSES

Overview: Data Analytics and Business Intelligence (BI) courses focus on developing skills in analyzing and interpreting data to make informed business decisions. These courses cover a range of topics, including data analysis, data visualization, statistical analysis, and data-driven decision-making. Here's an overview of these courses, how to join them, their eligibility requirements, and job opportunities:

Eligibility Requirements:
1. **Education:** Most programs require a minimum of a bachelor's degree in a relevant field such as computer science, engineering, mathematics, or business.
2. **Skills:** Proficiency in programming languages such as Python or R, as well as knowledge of statistical analysis and data visualization tools, may be required.

Job Opportunities:
1. **Data Analyst:** Analyze data to identify trends and patterns that can help businesses make informed decisions.
2. **Business Intelligence Analyst:** Use data analysis tools to develop reports, dashboards, and data visualizations to support business decision-making.
3. **Data Scientist:** Apply advanced statistical and machine learning techniques to analyze large datasets and derive insights.
4. **Business Analyst:** Analyze business processes and data to identify opportunities for improvement and growth.
5. **Data Engineer:** Design, build, and maintain data pipelines and infrastructure to support data analysis and BI initiatives.

SOME IMPORTANT SHORT TERM COURSES FOR BCOM STUDENTS

1. **Financial Modeling**: Learn how to create financial models and analyze financial statements, which is valuable for roles in finance, investment banking, and corporate finance.
2. **Advanced Excel**: Improve your proficiency in Excel, including functions, formulas, data analysis, and data visualization, which is useful in various business roles.
3. Business Analytics: Learn how to analyze data using statistical and analytical tools to make informed business decisions, which is valuable in roles involving data analysis and business intelligence.
4. **Foreign Language Courses**: Learning a foreign language such as Spanish, Mandarin, or French can enhance your global communication skills and broaden your career opportunities.
5. **Project Management**: Gain skills in project planning, execution, and management, which is valuable in roles involving project management or team leadership.

SOME IMPORTANT ARTIFICIAL INTELLIGENCE (AI) FOR BCOM STUDENTS

Studying Artificial Intelligence (AI) tools alongside a BCom degree can significantly enhance your skills and make you more competitive in the job market. Here are some important AI tools to consider studying:

1. **Python**: While not strictly an AI tool, Python is widely used in AI and data science due to its simplicity and readability. Learning Python will help you understand and implement AI algorithms.
2. **TensorFlow**: Developed by Google, TensorFlow is an open-source machine learning framework used for building and training neural network models.
3. **PyTorch**: Another popular open-source machine learning library, PyTorch is known for its flexibility and ease of use, especially for researchers and developers.
4. **Scikit-learn**: A simple and efficient tool for data mining and data analysis, Scikit-learn provides a range of machine learning algorithms for classification, regression, clustering, and more.
5. **Microsoft Azure Machine Learning**: Azure ML is a cloud-based service for building, training, and deploying machine learning models. It offers a range of tools and services for AI development.
6. **IBM Watson**: IBM Watson is a suite of AI tools and applications that use natural language processing and machine learning to provide insights and make predictions.
7. **Google Cloud AI Platform**: Google's AI Platform provides a range of tools and services for building and deploying machine learning models on Google Cloud.
8. **Amazon AI Services**: Amazon offers a range of AI services, including Amazon Lex for building conversational interfaces, Amazon Polly for text-to-speech, and Amazon Rekognition for image and video analysis.
9. **OpenCV**: OpenCV is an open-source computer vision and machine learning software library. It provides a range of tools and algorithms for image and video processing.

10. **NLTK (Natural Language Toolkit)**: NLTK is a leading platform for building Python programs to work with human language data. It provides easy-to-use interfaces to over 50 corpora and lexical resources.

These AI tools can help you develop valuable skills in AI and machine learning, which are increasingly in demand across industries. By learning these tools alongside your BCom degree, you can broaden your career opportunities and stay competitive in the rapidly evolving job market.

Conclusion:

The business world is evolving rapidly, driven by technological advancements and data-driven decision-making. By pursuing additional courses and certifications alongside your BCom degree, you position yourself at the forefront of this evolution. Whether it's mastering the principles of accounting, diving deep into data analytics, or exploring the potentials of AI, these additional qualifications will provide you with the tools and knowledge to succeed in a competitive and dynamic business landscape.

In this book, we have explored various courses and certifications that can be pursued alongside or after a BCom degree. Each path offers unique opportunities and advantages, tailored to different career aspirations and industry demands. By making informed choices and investing in continuous learning, you can build a robust and versatile career in the world of commerce.

www.ingramcontent.com/pod-product-compliance
Lightning Source LLC
Chambersburg PA
CBHW082241220526
45479CB00005B/1304